MOJITOS
MARTINIS & MARGARITAS

Printed in the United States of America
by G&R Publishing Co.

Distributed By:

507 Industrial Street
Waverly, IA 50677

ISBN-13: 978-1-56383-301-4
ISBN-10: 1-56383-301-8
Item #7091

S ince the early 1800s men and women alike have enjoyed a sip on the occasional cocktail.

Consisting of one or more types of liquor, flavorings, juice or spices, the cocktail gained true popularity from 1920 to 1933 when the sale and consumption of alcohol was outlawed. During this period, the art of mixing drinks was critical in order to mask the smell and taste of bootlegged alcohol.

Mixologists who developed their talents in illegal bars and speakeasies were heralded after the ban. The mid to late 1930s became known as the golden era of the cocktail.

Cocktails were made predominately with gin, whiskey or rum until the 1970s when the popularity of vodka increased and, by the 80s, became the prevailing base for mixed drinks.

Recently, we have entered a new era, the return of the true cocktail, with gin-based drinks like the Martini, rum-based drinks like the Mojito and brandy-based drinks like the Sidecar making huge comebacks.

From classic concoctions to new twists on old favorites and more, *Mojitos, Martinis and Margaritas* is filled with recipes for both the novice and experienced mixer.

The glossary on pages 4 and 5 is an introduction to common mixing terms, and drinkware descriptions are provided on pages 6 and 7 to help match each beverage to the proper glass. Take note of fun facts about traditional and new drinks as well as tips for serving and garnishing your concoctions.

Whether hosting a dinner party, relaxing at home or visiting the local watering hole, you're sure to find a cocktail to tickle your fancy.

Glossary

- **Build over ice:** To layer liquor or other cocktail ingredients in a glass filled with ice.

- **Dash:** To add a very small amount of an ingredient to a cocktail. There are 36 dashes in 1 ounce.

- **Float:** A small amount of liquor poured gently on top of a drink so it floats.

- **Fill:** To fill or pour liquid into glasses until it reaches the top or appropriate watermark. Usually designated for nonalcoholic mixers, such as juice or soda.

- **Frozen:** Ingredients are blended with ice until thick and smooth.

- **Garnish:** To decorate prepared cocktails with small colorful food items.

- **Muddle:** To mash, smash or crush ingredients with a spoon or muddler, which is a wooden or metal rod with a flattened end.

- **On the rocks:** A drink served over ice cubes.

- **Simple Syrup:** A mixture of sugar and water used in many cocktail recipes. To make, bring 2 cups of cold tap water to a boil. Stir in 2 cups of granulated sugar. Reduce the heat to
continued

low and stir constantly until the sugar dissolves completely. Allow to cool; transfer to a bottle or jar with a tight fitting lid and store in the refrigerator.

- **Splash:** To add a small amount of an ingredient to a cocktail. A splash is slightly larger than a dash, but still considered to be less than ½ ounce.

- **Straight up:** A drink served chilled but without ice.

- **Superfine sugar:** A type of sugar that dissolves well in cold or room temperature liquids, making it useful for cocktails. Superfine sugar's crystal size is the tiniest of all the types of granulated sugar. If you are unable to find superfine sugar, you can easily make your own by grinding granulated sugar in a food processor for 30 to 40 seconds.

Conversion Table

Ounce	(oz.)
Centiliter	(cl)
Milliliter	(ml)
Teaspoon	(tsp.)
Tablespoon	(T.)
Cup	(C.)

1 oz.	= 3 cl
1 oz.	= 30 ml
1 oz.	= 6 tsp.
1 oz.	= 2 T.

1 shot or jigger	= 1½ oz.
1 shot or jigger	= 4.5 cl
1 shot or jigger	= 45 ml

1 C.	= 8 oz.
1 C.	= 24 cl
1 C.	= 240 ml

Drinkware

Footed Cordial Glass
2 to 3 oz.

Champagne Flute
6 oz.

Champagne Saucer
4 oz.

Cocktail/Martini Glass – 4 oz.
* The martini glass is similar to the cocktail glass though the bowl is slightly less tapered, making it perfect to cradle an olive.

Collins Glass
8 to 12 oz.

Double Rocks Glass
12 oz.

Footed Highball Glass
8 to 12 oz.

Footed Rocks Glass
6 oz.

Highball Glass
8 to 12 oz.

Hurricane Glass
10 to 12 oz.

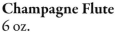
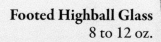
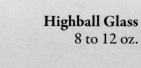

Brandy Snifter
6 to 12 oz.

Lowball Glass
4 to 6 oz.

Margarita Saucer
6 to 12 oz.

Old-Fashioned Glass
5 to 10 oz.

Poco Grande Glass
10 to 13 oz.

Red Wine Glass
6 to 8 oz.

Rocks Glass
6 oz.

Welled Margarita Glass
6 to 12 oz.

White Wine Glass
6 to 8 oz.

Cocktail Shaker
6 to 28 oz.

Ingredients

1 oz. crème de cassis

3 oz. Champagne

Cherry, optional

Kir Royal

Served: *Straight up*
Drinkware: *Champagne flute*

Pour the crème de cassis into the bottom of a Champagne flute. Top with Champagne and garnish with a cherry.

The Kir – made with white wine rather than Champagne – and the Kir Royal are named after Felix Kir, mayor of Dijon in Burgundy who popularized the drink by serving it at receptions to visiting delegates post-World War II. By doing so, he was not only delighting international guests, but also promoting two vital economic products of the region.

Ingredients
1 oz. lime juice
1½ oz. tequila
½ oz. triple sec
Lime slice, optional

Margarita

Served: *On the rocks*
Drinkware: *Welled margarita glass*

Fill a salt-rimmed margarita glass with ice and set aside. In a cocktail shaker filled with ice, combine lime juice, tequila and triple sec; shake vigorously. Strain into prepared margarita glass and garnish with lime slice. See page 39 for directions on rimming a glass with salt.

The margarita is served on the rocks or blended with ice to make a frozen margarita. The first frozen margarita machine was created by chemist John Hogan in 1971. He was recognized by the Smithsonian Institute for his invention.

Ingredients
2½ oz. gin
½ oz. dry vermouth
1 to 2 olives, optional

Dry Martini

Served: Straight up
Drinkware: Cocktail or martini glass

In a mixing glass filled with ice, stir together gin and vermouth. Strain into a chilled martini glass and garnish with olives.

The martini was favored by many legendary and historical figures in our culture, including Winston Churchill, Truman Capote, J. Robert Oppenheimer, F. Scott Fitzgerald, Ernest Hemingway, Cary Grant and President Franklin Delano Roosevelt.

Ingredients

1 oz. gin
1 oz. Campari
¾ oz. sweet vermouth
Burnt orange, optional

Negroni

Served: Straight up
Drinkware: Cocktail glass (shown in brandy snifter)

In a cocktail shaker filled with ice, combine the gin, Campari and sweet vermouth; shake vigorously. Strain into a chilled cocktail glass and garnish with burnt orange.

To make burnt orange, cut a 1½ x 1″ slice of peel off an orange. Be sure to get just the skin. Hold the peel over the glass between the thumb and index finger, with skin facing out. Light a match and hold it 1″ away from the peel; quickly squeeze the peel. If done correctly, a small burst of flame will ignite the secretion of the oils from the peel. Drop the twist into the drink to extinguish the flame.

Ingredients

½ fresh lime,
   cut into four wedges

1 tsp. sugar

2 oz. cachaca

Lime slice, opitonal

Caipirinha

Served: *On the rocks*
Drinkware: *Old-fashioned glass or rocks glass*

Place the lime wedges and sugar in an old-fashioned
glass and muddle. Fill the glass with crushed ice and
top with cachaca. Garnish with a lime slice.

*Pronounced "Kie-purr-REEN-yah", this refreshing drink is Brazil's
national cocktail. Caipirinha is the diminutive version of the word
"caipira", which refers to someone from the countryside.*

Ingredients

1 sugar cube
2 dashes of bitters
Splash of water
1 oz. Scotch
Lime wedge, orange slice
or 3 cherries, optional

Scotch Old-Fashioned

Served: *On the rocks*
Drinkware: *Old-fashioned glass*

Place sugar, bitters and water in an old-fashioned glass; muddle until sugar is dissolved. Fill the glass with ice cubes and top with Scotch. Garnish with a lime wedge, orange slice or cherries.

The Old-Fashioned is disputably the first drink ever referred to as a cocktail. It has been served since 1880 at the Pendennis Club in Louisville, Ky. Originally served with bourbon it was popularized by club member and bourbon distiller Colonel James E. Pepper who brought it to the Waldorf-Astoria Hotel bar in New York City.

Ingredients

1 medium ripe peach,
peeled and pureed

4 to 6 oz. Champagne

Peach slice, optional

Bellini

Served: *Straight up*
Drinkware: *Champagne flute*
(shown in white wine glass)

Pour peach puree into a Champagne flute. Slowly pour Champagne over puree; stir gently. Garnish with a peach slice.

Variation: To make a Bellini Martini, combine 2 oz. peach flavored vodka, 1 oz. peach puree and 1 oz. peach schnapps in an ice-filled cocktail shaker; shake vigorously. Strain into a chilled Champagne flute and add a splash of Champagne. Garnish with a peach slice.

Ingredients

1 oz. vodka

3 oz. orange juice

1 oz. Galliano

Cherries, orange twist
    or orange slice,
    optional

Harvey Wallbanger

Served: On the rocks
Drinkware: Highball or Collins glass

Fill a highball glass with ice and set aside. In a mixing glass, stir together vodka and orange juice. Strain mixture into the prepared glass. Top with Galliano and garnish with cherries, orange twist or orange slice.

The Harvey Wallbanger was first concocted in the 1950s by well-known mixologist Donato "Duke" Antone. Due to clever advertising by the importer of Galliano, the drink became so popular in the early 1970s that Harvey Wallbanger received thousands of write-in votes during the 1972 presidential election.

Ingredients

2 oz. tequila

4 oz. orange juice

1 oz. grenadine

Lime wedge or orange slice and cherry, optional

Tequila Sunrise

Served: On the rocks

Drinkware: Highball or Collins glass

Fill a highball glass with ice. Build over ice, beginning with tequila, then orange juice and finishing with grenadine. Do not stir. Garnish with a lime wedge or orange slice and cherry.

The Tequila Sunrise was originally served at the Arizona Biltmore Hotel and was named for the way it looks after prepared in a glass – the colors of the orange juice and grenadine mimic a sunrise.

Ingredients

2 oz. tequila
4 oz. orange juice
1 oz. blackberry brandy
Cherry, optional

Tequila Sunset

Served: *On the rocks*
Drinkware: *Highball (shown in cocktail glass)*

Fill a highball glass with ice. Build over ice, beginning with tequila, then orange juice and finishing with blackberry brandy. Do not stir. Garnish with a cherry.

"The problem with the world is that everyone is a few drinks behind."
– Humphrey Bogart

Ingredients

2 oz. vodka

1 oz. apple schnapps

Splash of lime juice

Apple slice, optional

Appletini

Served: Straight up
Drinkware: Cocktail or martini glass

In a cocktail shaker filled with ice, combine vodka, apple schnapps and lime juice; shake vigorously. Strain into a chilled martini glass and garnish with an apple slice.

Variation: To make a Sour Apple Martini, combine 2 oz. citrus vodka, ½ oz. sour apple schnapps, ½ oz. triple sec and ¾ oz. fresh lemon juice in an ice-filled cocktail shaker; shake vigorously. Strain into a chilled martini glass and garnish with an apple slice.

Ingredients

1 oz. vodka

1 oz. gin

1 oz. light rum

1 oz. tequila

1 oz. lemon juice

1 oz. triple sec

1 tsp. superfine sugar

3 oz. cola

Lemon wedge, optional

Long Island Iced Tea

Served: On the rocks
Drinkware: Highball or Collins glass

Fill a highball glass with ice. Combine vodka, gin, rum, tequila, lemon juice, triple sec, sugar and cola in the prepared glass. Stir until well combined. Garnish with a lemon wedge.

The origin of the Long Island Iced Tea is disputed.
Some believe the cocktail was invented during the Prohibition era
to take the appearance of a non-alcoholic drink. Other evidence
suggests the drink was first served in the late 1970s by bartender
Robert (Rosebud) Butt at the Oak Beach Inn in the
Town of Babylon, Long Island, New York.

Ingredients
1 oz. citrus vodka
½ oz. triple sec
½ oz. lime juice
1 oz. cranberry juice
Lime slice, optional

Cosmopolitan

Served: Straight up
Drinkware: Cocktail glass

In a cocktail shaker filled with ice, combine citrus vodka, triple sec, lime juice and cranberry juice; shake vigorously. Strain into a chilled cocktail glass and garnish with a lime slice.

The origin of the Cosmopolitan is somewhat disputed. South Beach, Florida bartender Cheryl Cook claims to have created the cocktail in 1985 or 1986. It gained popularity, traveling quickly from Miami to San Francisco to New York. The drink became even more well-known in the late 1990s with its frequent consumption by characters on the popular television series "Sex and the City."

Ingredients
2½ oz. gin
1½ tsp. sake
Olives, optional

Saketini

Served: *Straight up*
Drinkware: *Cocktail or martini glass*

In a mixing glass filled with ice, stir together gin and sake. Strain into a chilled martini glass and garnish with olives.

"I am prepared to believe that a dry martini slightly impairs the palate, but think what it does for the soul."

– *Alec Waugh*

Ingredients

1 oz. light rum
½ oz. orange curaçao
½ oz. Orgeat syrup
⅓ oz. lime juice
1 oz. dark rum
Pineapple wedge,
star fruit slice
and orange
slice, optional

Mai Tai

Served: *Straight up*
Drinkware: *Double rocks (shown in Collins glass)*

In a cocktail shaker filled with ice, combine light rum, orange curaçao, Orgeat syrup and lime juice; shake vigorously. Strain into a double rocks glass and float dark rum on top. Garnish with a pineapple wedge, star fruit slice and orange slice.

Victor J. Bergeron, also known as Trader Vic, invented the Mai Tai in 1944 at his Hinky Dinks restaurant in Oakland, Ca. After tasting the concoction, a Tahitian patron cried "Maita'i roa!" The literal translation being "good very", or figuratively "out of this world".

Ingredients

6 to 8 mint leaves

2 tsp. superfine sugar

1½ oz. lime juice

1½ oz. light rum

7 oz. soda water

Lime wedge and extra
   mint sprigs, optional

Mojito

Served: On the rocks
Drinkware: Collins glass

Place mint leaves, sugar and lime juice in a Collins glass and muddle. Fill glass with ice; add rum and stir until sugar is dissolved. Fill the glass with soda water and garnish with lime wedge and mint sprigs.

The mojito – pronounced "mo-HEE-toe" – is a traditional Cuban cocktail that became popular in the United States in the 1980s and has seen a recent resurgence in popularity with the emergence of new products such as mojito-flavored gum and beer.

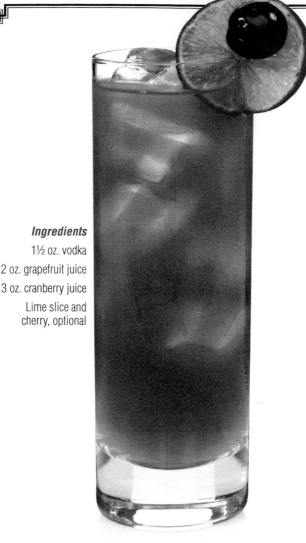

Ingredients
1½ oz. vodka
2 oz. grapefruit juice
3 oz. cranberry juice
Lime slice and
cherry, optional

Sea Breeze

Served: *On the rocks*
Drinkware: *Highball or Collins glass*

Fill a highball glass with ice and set aside. In a cocktail shaker filled with ice, combine vodka, grapefruit juice and cranberry juice; shake vigorously. Strain into the prepared glass and garnish with a lime slice and cherry.

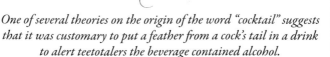

One of several theories on the origin of the word "cocktail" suggests that it was customary to put a feather from a cock's tail in a drink to alert teetotalers the beverage contained alcohol.

Ingredients

2 oz. vodka

½ oz. blue curaçao

4 oz. lemonade

Lemon wedge and
cherry, optional

Blue Lagoon

Served: On the rocks
Drinkware: Highball or Collins glass

Fill a highball glass halfway with ice. Build over ice, beginning with vodka and then blue curaçao. Top with lemonade and garnish with a lemon wedge and cherry.

"Drinking is a way of ending the day."
– Ernest Hemingway

Ingredients

1 oz. vodka
½ oz. coconut rum
1½ oz. pineapple juice
1½ oz. orange juice
Pineapple wedge,
optional

Malibu Beach

Served: *On the rocks*
Drinkware: *Collins or highball glass*

Fill a Collins glass with ice and set aside. In a cocktail shaker filled with ice, combine vodka, coconut rum, pineapple juice and orange juice; shake vigorously. Strain into the prepared glass and garnish with a pineapple wedge.

"Prohibition has made nothing but trouble."
– Al Capone

Ingredients

1 C. ice

1½ oz. tequila

½ oz. triple sec

Dash of lime juice

½ C. orange sherbet

Orange slice or mint leaves, optional

Orange Margarita

Served: Frozen

Drinkware: Welled margarita glass

Combine ice, tequila, triple sec, lime juice and orange sherbet in a blender; blend until smooth. Pour into a chilled margarita glass and garnish with orange slice or mint leaves.

Variation: To make a Kiwi Margarita, combine ½ C. ice, 2 oz. tequila, 2 oz. pineapple juice, 1 oz. triple sec, ½ oz. lime juice, 1 T. simple syrup and 1 kiwi fruit, peeled and quartered, in a blender; blend until smooth. Pour into a sugar-rimmed margarita glass and garnish with a slice of kiwi. See page 39 for directions on rimming glass with sugar.

Ingredients
2 oz. gin
1 oz. orange juice
1 tsp. superfine sugar
Orange slice or orange twist,
optional

Orange Blossom

Served: *Straight up*
Drinkware: *Cocktail or martini glass*

In a cocktail shaker filled with ice, combine gin,
orange juice and sugar; shake vigorously. Strain into a
chilled martini glass and garnish with an orange slice
or orange twist.

*Variation: To make an Orange Pomtini, combine 1½ oz.
pomegranate juice, 1½ oz. vodka and 1 oz. orange juice in a
cocktail shaker filled with ice; shake vigorously. Strain into a chilled
martini glass and garnish with pomegranate seeds.*

Ingredients

1½ oz. whiskey
¾ oz. triple sec
Dash of sour mix
½ oz. lime juice
7 oz. lemon-lime soda
Lime wedge, optional

Andreas

Served: On the rocks
Drinkware: Highball glass

Fill a highball glass with ice and set aside. In a cocktail shaker filled with ice, combine whiskey, triple sec, sour mix and lime juice; shake vigorously. Strain into the prepared glass and fill with lemon-lime soda. Garnish with a lime wedge.

"There can't be good living where there is not good drinking."
– Benjamin Franklin

Ingredients

3 oz. Galliano

1 oz. anise liqueur
or Pernod

7 oz. cola

2 to 3 lime wedges

Shocking Jack

Served: On the rocks
Drinkware: Highball glass

Fill a highball glass with ice. Build over ice, beginning with Galliano, then anise liqueur or Pernod. Fill with cola and add lime wedges.

Anise liqueur is produced from the anise plant. The plant, native to the Mediterranean, has small white flowers that bloom mid-summer followed by the growth of small licorice-flavored fruits call aniseed.

Ingredients
1 oz. vanilla vodka
1 oz. pineapple liqueur
7 oz. lemon-lime soda
Pineapple slice, optional

Vanilla Sky

Served: On the rocks
Drinkware: Highball glass

Fill a highball glass with ice and set aside. In a cocktail shaker filled with ice, combine the vanilla vodka and pineapple liqueur; shake vigorously. Strain into the prepared glass and fill with lemon-lime soda. Garnish with a pineapple slice.

"Never use water unless you have to! I'm going to use vermouth!"
– Julia Child

31

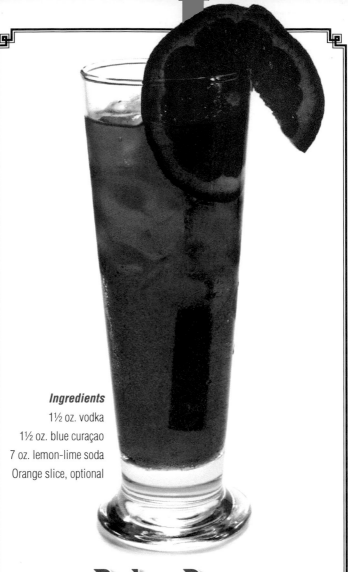

Ingredients
1½ oz. vodka
1½ oz. blue curaçao
7 oz. lemon-lime soda
Orange slice, optional

Polar Bear

Served: On the rocks
Drinkware: Highball or Collins glass

Fill a highball glass with ice. Build over ice, beginning with vodka, then blue curaçao. Fill with lemon-lime soda and garnish with an orange slice.

"In victory, you deserve Champagne. In defeat, you need it."
– Napoleon Bonaparte

Ingredients

1½ oz. gin

2 tsp. superfine sugar

1½ oz. lemon juice

4 oz. Champagne

Orange slice and
cherry, optional

French 75

Served: *On the rocks*
Drinkware: *Collins glass*

In a cocktail shaker filled with ice, combine gin,
superfine sugar and lemon juice; shake vigorously.
Strain into a Collins glass and fill with Champagne.
Garnish with an orange slice and cherry.

"I should never have switched from scotch to martinis."
— **Humphrey Bogart**

Ingredients
1½ oz. light rum
4 pineapple chunks
½ oz. lime juice
½ tsp. sugar
1 C. crushed ice
Pineapple slice, optional

Pineapple Daiquiri

Served: Frozen
Drinkware: Cocktail glass

Combine light rum, pineapple chunks, lime juice, sugar and crushed ice in a blender; blend on low until smooth. Pour into a cocktail glass and garnish with a pineapple slice.

Variation: To make a Mango Daiquiri, combine 1½ oz. light rum, 4 oz. mango juice, ½ oz. lime juice, ½ oz. triple see and 1 C. crushed ice cubes in a blender; blend on low until smooth. Pour into a hurricane glass and garnish with a cherry.

Ingredients

1½ oz. vodka

¾ oz. green crème de menthe

1½ oz. apple juice

3½ oz. soda water

Kiwi slice, optional

Russian Spring

Served: *On the rocks*
Drinkware: *Footed highball glass*

Fill a highball glass halfway with ice and set aside. In a cocktail shaker filled with ice, combine vodka, crème de menthe and apple juice; shake vigorously. Strain into the prepared glass and fill with soda water. Garnish with a kiwi slice.

"My only regret in life is that I did not drink more Champagne."
– John Maynard Keynes

Ingredients
1 oz. Hpnotiq
½ oz. raspberry liqueur
1 oz. raspberry vodka
Splash of pineapple juice

Blue Violet Martini

Served: Straight up
Drinkware: Cocktail or martini glass

In a mixing glass filled with ice, combine Hpnotiq, raspberry liqueur, raspberry vodka and pineapple juice; stir well. Strain into a chilled martini glass.

Variation: To make a Blue Fin, combine 2 oz. vodka, ¼ oz. lemon juice, ½ oz. Hpnotiq and 1 oz. white cranberry juice in a cocktail shaker filled with ice; shake vigorously. Strain into a chilled martini glass and garnish with lemon twist.

Ingredients

2 oz. Canadian whiskey
¾ oz. lime juice
1 T. simple syrup
1 tsp. grenadine
Cherry and orange twist, optional

New York

Served: *On the rocks*
Drinkware: *Old-fashioned glass*

Fill an old-fashioned glass with ice and set aside. In a cocktail shaker filled with ice, combine Canadian whiskey, lime juice, simple syrup and grenadine; shake vigorously. Strain into the prepared glass and garnish with a cherry and orange twist.

Another theory surrounding the origin of the word "cocktail" suggests cocktails were originally a morning beverage. The cocktail was the name given as a metaphor for the rooster, or cock, crowing at the break of dawn.

Ingredients

1 oz. vodka
¾ oz. raspberry liqueur
½ oz. lemon juice
Fresh raspberries, optional

French Horn

Served: *Straight up*
Drinkware: *Cordial glass (shown in cocktail glass)*

In a mixing glass filled with ice, combine vodka, raspberry liqueur and lemon juice; stir well. Strain into a cocktail glass and garnish with a few fresh raspberries.

*"The martini: the only American invention
as perfect as the sonnet."*

– H. L. Mencken

Ingredients

1½ oz. gin
1 tsp. grenadine
1 tsp. light cream
1 egg white
Cherry, optional

Pink Lady

Served: Straight up
Drinkware: Cocktail glass (shown in margarita saucer)

In a cocktail shaker filled with ice, combine gin, grenadine, light cream and egg white; shake vigorously. Strain into a sugar-rimmed margarita glass and garnish with a cherry.

Salt and sugar are most commonly used to rim a glass but some cocktails also work well with powdered sugar, crushed graham cracker or cocoa rimmed glasses. First, wet the outside rim of the glass with a fresh lemon or lime wedge. When rimming with sugar or cocoa, use one of the liquid ingredients, preferably a flavored liqueur. Place the sugar in a bowl or saucer and dip the moistened rim in the bowl.

Ingredients
1½ oz. gin
¾ oz. triple sec
¾ oz. lemon juice
Lime slice, optional

White Lady

Served: Straight up
Drinkware: Cocktail glass

In a cocktail shaker filled with ice, combine the gin, triple sec and lemon juice; shake vigorously. Strain into a chilled cocktail glass or sugar-rimmed cocktail glass. Garnish with lime slice. See page 39 for directions on rimming a glass with sugar.

Variation: To make a Sidecar, combine 2 oz. brandy, 2 oz. triple sec and ½ oz. lemon juice in an ice-filled cocktail shaker; shake vigorously. Strain into a chilled cocktail glass and garnish with an orange wedge.

Ingredients

1½ oz. Canadian whiskey

½ oz. triple sec

2 drops Angostura bitters

Mint sprig, optional

Canadian

Served: On the rocks
Drinkware: Old-fashioned or footed rocks glass

Fill a rocks glass with ice. Add Canadian whiskey, triple sec and Angostura bitters to prepared glass; stir. Garnish with mint sprig.

Canadian whiskey that is made in Canada, by law, must be aged at least three years in a wooden barrel. Canadian whiskies are blended multi-grain whiskies. They are usually lighter and smoother than other styles.

Ingredients

3 oz. Champagne
1 oz. grapefruit juice
1 oz. pineapple juice
1 tsp. grenadine
Cherry and mint sprig,
optional

Ritz Bar Fizz

Served: Straight up
Drinkware: Champagne saucer

Pour Champagne, grapefruit juice, pineapple juice and
grenadine into a Champagne saucer; stir to combine.
Garnish with a cherry and mint sprig.

Variation: To make a London Bus, pour 3 oz. Champagne,
1 oz. mandarin juice, 1 oz. grapefruit juice and 1 tsp. passion-fruit
syrup into a Champagne saucer; stir to combine.

Ingredients

1½ oz. vodka

1½ oz. lychee or lichti liqueur

Dash of lime juice

Pitted lychee fruit, optional

Lychee Martini

Served: *Straight up*
Drinkware: *Cocktail or martini glass*

In a cocktail shaker filled with ice, combine vodka, lychee or lichti liqueur and lime juice; shake vigorously. Strain into a chilled martini glass and garnish with a pitted lychee fruit.

The lychee or lichti fruit is a tropical fruit tree native to southern China. It is also found in India, northern Vietnam, Indonesia and the Philippines. The super sweet fruit is sold fresh in Vietnamese, Chinese and Asian markets and began appearing in supermarkets in recent years.

Ingredients
1 oz. vodka
2 oz. pineapple juice
2 oz. Champagne
Pineapple wedge, optional

Flirtini

Served: Straight up
Drinkware: Cocktail or martini glass

In a cocktail shaker filled with ice, combine vodka and pineapple juice; shake vigorously. Strain into a chilled martini glass and top with Champagne. Garnish with a pineapple wedge.

The makers of Champagne are fiercely protective of the wine that made their region famous. Therefore, most bottles labeled Champagne come from this northern French region. Most "champagnes" produced elsewhere must be labeled as sparkling wine.

Ingredients

1 C. crushed ice
2 oz. tequila
½ oz. triple sec
2 oz. grapefruit juice
½ oz. grenadine
Orange slice and cherry,
  optional

Icebreaker

Served: On the rocks
Drinkware: *White or Red wine glass*

Combine crushed ice, tequila, triple sec, grapefruit juice and grenadine in a blender; blend on low for 12 seconds. Strain into a sugar-rimmed wine glass and garnish with an orange slice and cherry. See page 39 for directions on rimming a glass with sugar.

*"Remember please, that a too-sweet daiquiri
is like a lovely lady with too much perfume."*
    – **Charles Baker**

Ingredients
2 oz. vanilla vodka
½ oz. triple sec
2½ oz. pineapple juice
½ oz. lime cordial
½ oz. lime juice

Key Lime Pie

Served: Straight up
Drinkware: Cocktail or martini glass

In a cocktail shaker filled with ice, combine vanilla vodka, triple sec, pineapple juice, lime cordial and lime juice; shake vigorously. Strain into a chilled martini glass or a crushed graham cracker-rimmed martini glass. See page 39 for directions on rimming a glass with crushed graham crackers.

Ingredients

1 oz. Hpnotiq
2 oz. light rum
6 to 8 mint leaves
3 oz. soda water
Mint sprig, optional

Blue Mojito

Served: *On the rocks*
Drinkware: *Collins glass*

Fill a Collins glass with ice and set aside. In a cocktail shaker filled with ice, combine Hpnotiq, light rum and mint leaves; shake vigorously. Strain into prepared Collins glass and top with soda water. Garnish with a mint sprig.

Variation: To make a Blueberry Mojito, muddle 8 mint leaves with 1 tsp. sugar in a Collins glass. Fill glass with ice and add 1½ oz. light rum and ¼ oz. lime juice. Fill with soda water and drop in 8 fresh blueberries.

Ingredients
2½ oz. Scotch
1 oz. sweet vermouth
Dash of Angostura bitters

Rob Roy

Served: *Straight up*
Drinkware: *Cocktail glass*

In a mixing glass filled with ice, combine Scotch, sweet vermouth and Angostura bitters; stir well. Strain into a chilled cocktail glass.

The Rob Roy was first introduced at the Waldorf Astoria in 1894 in honor of the opening of the Broadway play of the same name. The play was about Robert Roy MacGregor, the Scottish Robin Hood of the 18th century.

Ingredients

1¼ oz. spiced rum

1½ oz. orange juice

1½ oz. pineapple juice

1 oz. sweet and sour mix

½ oz. dark rum

Pineapple wedge and cherry, optional

Jamaican Sunset

Served: *On the rocks*
Drinkware: *Hurricane glass*

Fill a hurricane glass with ice and set aside. In a cocktail shaker filled with ice, combine spiced rum, orange juice, pineapple juice, and sweet and sour mix; shake vigorously. Strain into prepared glass and float dark rum on top. Garnish with a pineapple wedge and cherry.

*"Gimme a whiskey, ginger ale on the side.
And don't be stingy, baby."*
— *Greta Garbo*

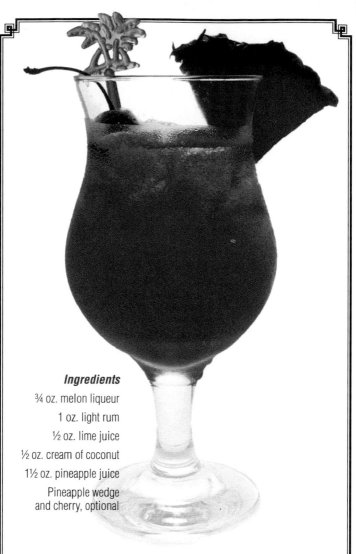

Ingredients

¾ oz. melon liqueur

1 oz. light rum

½ oz. lime juice

½ oz. cream of coconut

1½ oz. pineapple juice

Pineapple wedge
and cherry, optional

Green Eyes

Served: *On the rocks or frozen*
Drinkware: *Poco Grande glass*

Fill a Poco Grande glass with crushed ice. Pour melon liqueur, rum, lime juice, cream of coconut and pineapple juice over ice; stir well. Garnish with a pineapple wedge and cherry.

Ingredients

1½ oz. green crème de menthe

1½ oz. vodka

1½ oz. light rum

Mint sprig and kiwi slice, optional

Mint Haze

Served: On the rocks
Drinkware: Old-fashioned glass

Fill an old-fashioned glass halfway with crushed ice. Build over ice, beginning with the crème de menthe, then vodka and finishing with rum. Stir and garnish with mint sprig and kiwi slice.

Ingredients

1 C. crushed ice
1 oz. light rum
2 oz. pineapple juice
1 oz. blue curaçao
1 oz. cream of coconut
Pineapple wedge
and cherry, optional

Blue Hawaii

Served: *Frozen*
Drinkware: *Hurricane glass*

Combine ice, light rum, pineapple juice, blue curaçao
and cream of coconut in a blender; blend on high until
smooth. Pour into a hurricane glass and garnish with a
pineapple wedge and cherry.

Ingredients

1½ tsp. apricot brandy
2 oz. vodka
½ oz. lime juice
7 oz. soda water
½ banana, sliced
Mint sprig, optional

Banana Punch

Served: *On the rocks*
Drinkware: *Poco Grande glass*

Fill a Poco Grande glass with crushed ice. Pour apricot brandy, vodka and lime juice over ice; stir well. Fill with soda water and stir. Add banana slices and garnish with a mint sprig.

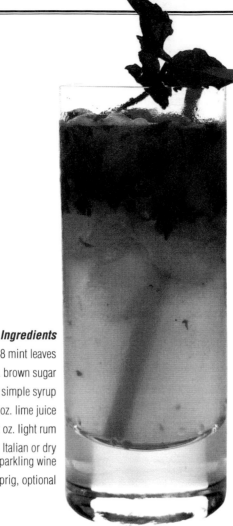

Ingredients

6 to 8 mint leaves
1 tsp. brown sugar
1 tsp. simple syrup
½ oz. lime juice
2 oz. light rum
2 oz. Italian or dry
sparkling wine
Mint sprig, optional

Italian Mojito

Served: *On the rocks*
Drinkware: *Collins glass*

Place mint leaves, brown sugar, simple syrup and lime juice in a Collins glass and muddle. Fill glass with ice cubes and pour in light rum. Top with sparkling wine and garnish with a mint sprig.

Ingredients

2½ oz. light rum
1 oz. lime juice
1 T. simple syrup
Lemon slice, optional

Classic Daiquiri

Served: Straight up
Drinkware: Cocktail glass

In a cocktail shaker filled with ice, combine light rum,
lime juice and simple syrup; shake vigorously. Strain into
a chilled cocktail glass and garnish with a lemon slice.

*To present this cocktail with flair, garnish with a floating
lemon slice topped with shaved or crushed ice. To create this effect,
place or float the lemon slice on top of the prepared cocktail.
In a blender, blend 2 to 3 ice cubes on low until ice is the
consistency of snow. Gently place ½ tablespoon of shaved
or crushed ice on top of the lemon slice.*

Ingredients

1¾ oz. gold rum
¼ oz. dark crème de cacao
½ oz. lime juice

Mulata

Served: *On the rocks*
Drinkware: *Welled margarita glass*

Fill a margarita glass with crushed ice and set aside.
In a cocktail shaker filled with ice, combine gold rum,
crème de cacao and lime juice; shake vigorously. Strain
into the prepared glass.

*Crème de cacao is a sweet chocolate liqueur. It is flavored primarily
by the cocoa bean and vanilla orchid.*

Ingredients

1 oz. sweet vermouth

1 oz. Campari

Dash of soda water

Orange slice or lemon peel, optional

Americano

Served: On the rocks
Drinkware: Collins glass

Fill a Collins glass with ice and set aside. In a cocktail shaker filled with ice, combine sweet vermouth, Campari and soda water; shake vigorously. Strain mixture into prepared Collins glass and garnish with an orange slice or lemon peel.

The Americano was first served in Gaspare Campari's Milan, Italy bar in the 1860s. The cocktail was originally named the Milano-Torina, but in the early 1900s Italians noticed a surge in Americans consuming the cocktail. It eventually became known as the Americano.

Ingredients

2 oz. bourbon

¼ oz. sweet vermouth

3 dashes of bitters

Orange slice and cherry, optional

Manhattan

Served: Straight up
Drinkware: Cocktail glass

In a cocktail shaker filled with ice, combine bourbon, sweet vermouth and bitters; shake vigorously. Strain into a chilled cocktail glass and garnish with an orange slice and a cherry. For directions on garnishing with a floating orange and shaved ice, see page 55.

Index

Tequila

Icebreaker	45
Kiwi Margarita	27
Long Island Iced Tea	19
Margarita	9
Orange Margarita	27
Tequila Sunrise	16
Tequila Sunset	17

Vodka

Appletini	18
Banana Punch	53
Bellini Martini	14
Blue Fin	36
Blue Lagoon	25
Blue Violet Martini	36
Cosmopolitan	20
Flirtini	44
French Horn	38
Harvey Wallbanger	15
Key Lime Pie	46
Long Island Iced Tea	19
Lychee Martini	43
Malibu Beach	26
Mint Haze	51
Orange Pomtini	28
Polar Bear	32
Russian Spring	35
Sea Breeze	24
Sour Apple Martini	18
Vanilla Sky	31

Whiskey

Andreas	29
Canadian	41
Manhattan	58
New York	37
Rob Roy	48
Scotch Old-Fashioned	13

Other

Blue Violet Martini	36
Caipirinha	12
Saketini	21
Shocking Jack	30
Sidecar	40